I HAVE AUTISM, AND IT'S OKAY!

Written by
Dr. William M. Bauer

Illustrated by
Mallory Hill

WestBow Press books may be ordered through booksellers or by contacting:

WestBow Press
A Division of Thomas Nelson & Zondervan
1663 Liberty Drive
Bloomington, IN 47403
www.westbowpress.com
844-714-3454

Interior Image Credit: Mallory Hill

ISBN: 978-1-6642-4350-7 (sc)
ISBN: 978-1-6642-4351-4 (e)

Library of Congress Control Number: 2021912589

Print information available on the last page.

WestBow Press rev. date: 09/13/2021

WestBow
PRESS®
A DIVISION OF THOMAS NELSON
& ZONDERVAN

I HAVE AUTISM, AND
IT'S OKAY!

About the Author:

Dr. William M. (Bill) Bauer is a licensed clinical counselor in the rural Mid-Ohio Valley area who was a former classroom teacher, principal, and college professor. He has worked with children and adults with disabilities all of his life and hopes that this book brings an understanding to children with disabilities, their teachers, and their classmates. Dr. Bauer was born with a severe hearing impairment.

THIS BOOK IS DEDICATED TO:

ALL PEOPLE WITH DISABILITIES WHOSE LIVES ARE SHARED IN THIS BOOK SERIES TO MAKE THE WORLD A BETTER PLACE. ALL WE WANT IS TO BE ACCEPTED AS WE ARE, HAVE FRIENDS, LIVE IN OUR COMMUNITIES AND TO DREAM AS OUR NON-DISABLED PEERS.

SPECIAL THANKS TO MY WIFE, MARY ELLA, DAUGHTER MADISON RYSER, HER HUSBAND ANDREW AND GRANDSON JACK.

#GRANTSPEED. LOVE YOU, SON

Forewords:

I have had the pleasure of working with Dr. Bauer in the professional education and mental health fields for over two decades, and this book series is his latest outstanding work to help young people understand and accept differences. Each title focuses on a uniqueness and assures us that "it is OKAY!"

Dr. Stephanie Starcher
Public School Superintendent

Being different is OK! Every effort to erase stigma surrounding our differences is important. The earlier we start, the better chance we have at preventing stigma from even occurring. I had the honor of meeting Dr. Bill Bauer when I was in college, and it is no surprise his work as a mental health advocate would transpire into this series of books. I'm thankful for his commitment to celebrating our differences.

Nick Gehlfuss, MFA, Actor, film and television.
Currently, Dr. Halstead, Chicago Med.

This book series by Dr. William Bauer – my good friend Bill – fills a niche in children's literature that embraces diversity and self esteem. This series is not only important, but extremely fun. As founder of Orphans International, I look forward to reading these stories to children of all faiths and abilities around the world. This book is indeed a living testament to Bill's own son. The world is a better place because of Bill Bauer! #GrantSpeed

James Jay Dudley Luce, Founder Orphans International Worldwide,
International Entrepreneur

HI!

MY NAME IS CARSYN, AND I HAVE AUTISM.

AUTISM COMES IN ALL SHAPES AND SIZES, LIKE PIECES OF A PUZZLE.

THERE IS NO ONE TYPE OF AUTISM. EACH PERSON WHO HAS AUTISM IS DIFFERENT FROM THE OTHER PERSON.

MOST PEOPLE WITH AUTISM DO NOT LIKE TO TALK TO PEOPLE OR JUST FEEL DIFFERENT WHEN THEY DO.

SOME PEOPLE WITH AUTISM ARE VERY SMART IN ONE AREA OR SHOW GREAT SKILLS IN ONE OR TWO AREAS.

SOMETIMES I FEEL LIKE I AM ON A DIFFERENT PLANET AND SOME RULES DON'T MAKE SENSE TO ME. I NEED PEOPLE TO HELP ME UNDERSTAND.

WHEN THINGS HAPPEN OUT OF ORDER AND NOT THE WAY THINGS ARE SUPPOSED TO HAPPEN, I SOMETIMES MELT DOWN UNTIL SOMEONE HELPS ME CALM DOWN.

IT IS A GOOD THING TO LET ME KNOW WHEN THINGS ARE CHANGING AHEAD OF TIME SO THAT I CAN GET READY FOR THE CHANGE. CHANGE IS HARD FOR ME. LOUD NOISES, SOMETHINGS I TOUCH AND SOME TASTES ARE HARD FOR ME. SOMETIMES I EAT THE SAME THING OVER AND OVER.

AT SCHOOL, SOMETIMES I HAVE TO GO TO A DIFFERENT ROOM TO LEARN OR JUST TO CALM MYSELF DOWN.

I LIKE MY FRIENDS WHO ACCEPT ME FOR WHO I AM AND CAN UNDERSTAND ME.

My name is Carsyn. I have Autism, and it's okay!

Printed in the United States
by Baker & Taylor Publisher Services